This diary belongs to

www.ingramcontent.com/pod-product-compliance
Lightning Source LLC
Chambersburg PA
CBHW070834310526
45788CB00017B/939
* 9 7 8 1 0 9 4 9 2 4 1 9 9 *